Psychology Of Color...

Jesse Charles Fremont Grumbine

CONTENTS

CHAPTER I.

PSYCHOLOGY AS APPLIED TO SUPERSENSITIVENESS AND THE FINER EFFLUENCES OF MATTER.

Science is showing how much finer, thinner, more impenetrable, denser in electrical and chemical substance and tenuity the ether is than any known gas. Indeed, it is more and more believed that matter in all its infinite forms stands up under so many kinds of conditions which demand other more highly developed and, perhaps, differently constituted functions of the human mind to apprehend and perceive them.

To use any of the five senses, with which the normal man is equipped, is the most natural process in the world, but to transcend this use, to see, as the cat, and smell as the dog, depend upon specialization of a sense beyond its normal use. That the cat and dog have the sense of sight and smell, extended in power, is true, but it is also true that this same specialized organ could not be made available, if it were not for the finer particles of matter, which their organs detect, but which make no impression on the ordinary senses of man. For the lack of a better word to express this finer chemical matter, the word effluence is employed. Matter is in a state of disintegration. Particles are separating from the gross, compact mass all the time. Chemical combination is opposed by chemical segregation.

No matter is really at rest. It may appear superficially at rest, but this is only a passing phenomenon of its transition. Its electrons are in a perpetual whirl of high speed vortices. Steel is eaten up by the acids of the atmosphere, and the granitic rocks dissolve under similar attritions. The dust of the universe, held together by attraction, is separated by repulsion, and science has not yet been able to find its concrete resting place. It passes through the three dimensions into the fourth, and back again without betraying the occult secret. And yet not, however, without imparting an effluence, which is matter's ghostly shadow which betrays its invisible presence. This effluence may be called an emanation. It is not without its appeal to the mind, although the mind may not consciously sense it. Now, in order to perceive the presence of these finer particles of matter, and know of their existence, it is only necessary to pass from ordinary sense perception, to the supersensuous, called supersensitiveness. This sense development or culture is not attained except under certain conditions. Fortunately, there are many who are born clairsentiently*, that is, who are able to feel, see, hear, smell, taste, what to the average man is unknown. It is due in part, not only to the virility and virtue of the senses, but to an aloofness or separation from vicious indulgences. The person whose several senses are kept pure and clean has the advantage over one who is interested more in sensations or the pleasures which they afford than in their higher uses.

To vitiate or deprave the senses is to force a condition upon mental faculties and processes which inhibit and sometimes atrophy them to higher and more sublime impressions. This is why abstemiousness is preferred to indulgence. A sense can be corrupted as easily as a moral action. So when the effluences of matter impress the sensory the mind should be sufficiently sensitized to permit whatever sense is employed in any given perception to have a clear right of way. Obstructions which are inherent in mind, are more fatal to results than alien or external physical influences such as are apt to disturb a perfect concentration. Supersensitiveness becomes in time a habit.

---

*Clairsentiently is here used to express acute sensitiveness of a supernormal character.

Partial subjectification of one's senses, that is, applying them to perceive these finer forces and effluences of matter, which are extremely delicate and unobtrusive in their impact upon the sensory is necessary and inevitable. Each sense must be rendered acute—that is, as perfect in its service as it is possible, before one can hope to perceive the finer emanations. No sense is made more alive by destruction. Habitual employment of one's senses in an unrestricted attention to their value, efficiency and sublime service to the soul, will accomplish wonders. When it is understood, as it will be with the widespread publication of the findings of the Psychical Research Society that as Dr. Anna Bonus Kingsford wrote over fifty years ago, "Matter in its grossest form is the last term of a descending category", we shall not limit the descending or ascending scale of variable forms of matter which co-ordinate with the equally different conditions, states and functions of consciousness, but will be watchful as well as careful of their connections and inter-relations and observe how the interior expression of life and intelligence modifies the forms in which they manifest. In this way, effects can be perceived, analyzed, tabulated, and a theory at last advanced which will explain the unity of natural and spiritual law.

The interpenetration of matter by the ether, is no less true of force, life and spirit. How, is yet to be discovered. Science is dangerously near the secret, if not the solution. Professor Thompson has shown how very illusive and thin is the partition between electrons and super energy, which he does not call mind or spirit, but which physical science is slowly admitting to be in the ascending category of "energy." However, potential energy is with life and intelligence, its most remarkable attributes if such they may be termed, is its seemingly dualistic and yet harmonial and unitary nature. Is there any possible definition of "matter" that can define "mind", or "mind" that can define "matter"? And yet in the natural world, these two forms of the one and same energy interplay in a symphony of life, at once complete and divine. This energy is more than force and for the lack of a scientific word which will convey its compliments of power it is called, "Divinity." In the word "Divinity," there is all that is comprehended by the word spirit, soul, intelligence, mind, life, personality, form, matter; for Divinity is not less than the least, but greater than the greatest of its evolutions or expressions. Therefore, the adaptability and elasticity of matter are not properties or potentialities of matter, as matter is understood, but modes of the manifestation and expression of Divinity. So that, if one is dealing with the effluences of matter, or the supersensitiveness of mind, both are within the function and sphere of Divinity; and, it is for the Divinity to perceive, not only its own prerogatives, to know its own states and planes of consciousness and life, but to realize that there is a unity of free, intelligent action between what seems within (function, sensitiveness, mind) and without (organism, matter, effluence). Psychology is showing that however pragmatic the operations and acts of the normal and supernormal powers of the mind should be, action alone cannot gauge, determine or reveal all that is within, above and beyond mind and yet of Divinity. Do not imagine that there is any mystery implied in this statement or use of the word. On the contrary, there is so eminent an authority as Ralph Waldo Emerson, who, confronting the same reality, declared that "there is that which is, but can never become, and that which is becoming but can never be;" and Dr. C. S. Whitly in his essay on Leibnitz remarks that "the essence of things is too intangible to be caught in the coarse meshes of human logic." Backunin says "Science comprehends the thought of reality; not reality itself, the thought of life, not life." So, however occult matter and life are or however organism and mind or personality and Divinity are related, nothing supernatural or mysterious is implied by the connection. It is nature on another plane of experimental expression, Burbanking her latent, but potential powers in a dualistic relationship, without in any sense, interrupting or destroying any lower, normal, mental or physical expression of the unity of life. Physical senses perceive physical objects through physical sensations and form mental concepts, accordingly. The gamut of sensations, measures coarse and dynamic as well as fine and static impressions. As a whole they are grouped under sense perceptions. They are known through the sensory. They are of the objective, normal mind. But there are other impressions that may fill the gap between the lowest audible and visible vibrations, and the ether, and which we know exist, as for instance, the ultra violet and infra red rays which can be detected by chemical processes. These can also be felt and detected by and through one's Divinity without resorting to external, physical apparatus. Supersensitiveness is the film which snaps these impressions and gives it to the mind, when it is ready to develop it. Without supersensitiveness, these effluences could not be caught or imprisoned by the mind, and the keener and finer is one's sensitiveness, that is the more it becomes supernormal, the less likely are these impressions to be denied or neglected or lost. Academically, psychology has stood in its own light for over a century, despite the rapid accumulation of new and strange occult facts which have forced upon it a new view point. Despite, also, the verdict of men of science concerning the spiritual origin of mind as well as the universe. Must the mind be abandoned as plane after plane of finer matter is discovered and exposed to view? Must it be forgotten that mind has no place in this interior or finer field of forces to function on its own account, to explore this field of effluences, which belong rightly to the sphere of its supernormal powers as embraced in the word, supersensitiveness?

Every object in nature is enveloped in an aura or cloud of emanations, which seems to be its field of action. It discharges this aura by chemical attraction and disintegration. Conscious intelligence parallels and responds to every form of matter, and whether gross or coarse or fine, no outer excitation or stimulus fails to make a record on the nerve and sense centres of perception. More than this. The impression is reflected, so that however dynamic or delicate and unobtrusive it may be originally, the secondary effect is not lost. As the infra red and ultra violet rays produce effects upon life, which cannot be measured or determined as are the primary colors by usual, mechanical or chemical processes, but need an instrument peculiarly fitted as is the bolometre for detecting the infra red rays, and the fluroscope for detecting the ultra violet, so these phychological effects can only be gotten at by the employment of supernormal powers—normal powers so trained, deepened and purified, so that the sensitive perception can apprehend them. Thus graded forms of matter from the solid to the electrical and etheric, relate to life and consciousness on the ascending scale of sublimated psychic powers. The sharp, concrete line cannot, of course, be drawn experimentally between normal and supernormal powers, except to show in practice that the normal are the potential supernormal and the supernormal are the latent normal powers; which means, that when the supernormal powers are active, they are normal, and when the normal powers are active, the supernormal are passive or inactive. For experimentally, the supernormal use of any normal power is different, not because it is an infringement of natural law, but because it is tracing the grosser impact of sensation on the sensory, not through memory, or a cognition of the physical sense perception, but through the perception or feeling of the finer effects which cannot be detected by the physical senses at all. This is in part the function of the subjective or what the late Dr. Frederick Myers called "the subliminal mind," in contra distinction to "supraliminal mind." This eliminates mystery or miracle from the psychological process, and proves it to be scientific, because demonstrably pragmatic. Thousands of cases could be cited of how these emanations of matter which are so impossible to get at by any known physical process, and yet, suffuse the forms of things, are discovered by anyone whose supernormal power of sensitiveness (super sensitiveness) has become active even to a small degree. For instance, however uncanny or impossible the facts may be, it is a common experience, that in certain houses, where crime has been committed, a sensitive person feels the "atmosphere" of the criminal, as well as the emanations, which the criminal's aura, and the physical struggle of a victim imparted to the room, in which the deed was committed, and that too, without knowing that any crime had taken place. The wall, pictures, carpets, furniture, even the room bespeaks the horror of the crime. This

may occur years after the act took place, and
even if the room should be empty, re-papered or
refurnished. Emanations are so powerfully
present and vital to the consciousness that can.
apprehend them. One dislikes a street, or a lo-
cality, houses or things, not because of any out-
ward ugliness in appearance, but because some
sinister influence of one person or a number of
persons, quite unknown to the sensitive, has im-
pregnated them with what is so unpleasantly and
disagreeably repulsive. Insomnia, restlessness,
fear, horror of impending disaster may come
to any one at night who, resting on a pillow or
bed, in a hotel or a home, in which a previous
guest, or guests were thus mentally disturbed.
These emanations discharged from the human
personality in subtile forms of matter adhere to
objects, and even time, the great healer, cannot
erase the effects. Involved negatives of these
finer, kinetic influences adhere in the soul or
substance of matter, and what hitherto has been
tabooed by science or regarded as superstition,
is at last proven to be neither occult, nor supernatural, but a neglected field of finer vibrations,
too delicately unobtrusive to be detected except
by supersensitiveness.

Color, in its appeal to the human mind, affects
nerve and emotional centers through its efflu-

ences and these finer wave lengths of energy are perceived and their influence felt by that function of the soul which is supersensitiveness, which belongs to each one and is his psychic endowment, however unconscious he may be of it.

Perhaps, upon very close analytical scrutiny, it will be found that the psychology of this psychic supersensitiveness will reveal a co-ordination of color vibrations to moral impulses, so that there will be shown an ethical side to color, which hitherto has been but faintly or indefinitely appreciated. So that good or evil, moral and immoral effects may be involved in every human perception of physical light as light is reflected in color. However, involved and illusive the ethical side of the psychology of color is, the effect of color on the morals of man is self-evident.

What is true of color is also true of sound. The moral quality must not be associated with the mere sensation and perception of the pleasure or pain which color may produce. In highly organized or sensitized bodies, high, medium or low pitch of sound waves produce proportionately painful and pleasurable effects, as witness as shown by Mr. Aitken in his book on "THE FIVE WINDOWS OF THE SOUL," how reptiles and scorpions writhe in pain when the notes of a piccolo are sounded and become enchanted when the flute is played. To a serpent, a piccolo would be an instrument of torture and he would attack and kill under its influence. The moral effect on the reptile is to make it ill behaved, that is bad; on the contrary, the flute would iron out its wrinkled coils, subdue its temper, soothe its nervous system and so cause it to be well behaved, that is good.

Similarly, some forms of color excitation intensify the sensation of pain and the moral effect is bad, while other forms soothe the nerves and the moral effect is good. This is especially significant in the therapeutic and pathological values of the various forms of electrical discharge as the violet rays which overcome, to an extent more and more appreciated by chromopathologists and electro therapeuticists, functional and organic diseases. Dr. Edward Babbit in his pioneer work on "The Philosophy of Light" furnishes unquestionable evidences of the beneficial and healing quality of color.

Color in nature is not only ornamental, but useful. It serves a purpose in vegetable, insect, bird, fish and all animal life which is not only offensive and defensive, and hence protective, but contributes valuable suggestions relative to the nature and habits of the species along lines of struggle and survival.

If red, flaunted in the face of a bull infuriates the beast, surely, the effect is none the less dynamic and hostile though not so spontaneous, among men and women of low or elemental natures. For red is thermal, a stimulus, an irritant, a fiery energy which arouses the blood and passion of the animal nature, whether in beast or man, while blue is a counter irritant, is depressing, electrical and soothing in its effect upon the nerves. Blue is an antidote for the effects of red, as red is an antidote for the effects of blue. A neutralizing effect of red or blue is produced by the red or blue being modified by white. The purer the color, that is, the more transparent it is the more forceful is its vibrations. The more a color is tinctured with matter of coarser substance or slower vibrations, the more mixed and confusing is its effect upon the sensory.

Color is both physical, (that is chemical) and psychological (mental) in its effect upon the mind. The chemical effect is a nervous one; the psychological effect is psychic. The nervous system reflects its disturbances upon the mind, hence the sensation of pain and pleasure, and the emotional states which accompany them. This is true of all the colors. Primary colors are radical, elemental and fixed in their vibrations or wave lengths, and hence, when once the effects of the sensations which they produce on the mind are known, their uniformity can always be depended upon. Red as thermal and a stimulent, and blue as electrical and depressing, act uniformly on all forms of life. So with yellow. Light by the spectrum analysis proves that its seven colors are made up of vibrations or wave lengths of mathematical exactness. If the seven colors are modified in any way whatsoever, this mathematical condition or unity is disturbed and disarranged, and the effect upon the senses will be determined by the alien substance which causes the modification. The difference can be gotten as much by calculation as by subtle, psychological analysis. For instance, the effect of pink is different from light blue. Pink or red in any form is a physical stimulant to the sensibilities, while blue is a physical depressant, but a spiritual inspiration, so that by blue or its modifications, a cooling influence or feeling is obtained, while by the red a warming influence or feeling follows. Surely, therefore, if one is trying to get these two opposite effects he will be careful to use the correct one.

As chromopathically applied one given to exaggeration or falsification, should be treated with blue and often the brilliant blues of turquoise, Italian or peacock blue, or Alice blue work more quickly and efficaciously than the lighter effects. Children who with active imaginations are apt to exaggerate or tell stories, with only fancy for the foundation, should have for a nursery a blue room and at night should be put to sleep in a bed room papered in a delicate shade of blue and be covered with a blue comforter. On the contrary, a child that is very sober, thoughtful, spiritual, or even matter of fact, should have a pink papered play room, with a bedroom decorated with pink roses and be covered with a pink comforter. It will at once be perceived why white and delicate tints of blue and red are mostly chosen for children. The choice is not accidental, but deeply rooted in a mother's intuition or instinct of what is most helpful and appealing to a child. Just red or blue might be most irritating. This would be so to various individualized children. White, because of its suggestiveness of purity and cleanliness, having all colors latent in its form, while pink, arousing gentle heat waves and so expressing and impressing the emotional quality of love and amiability, while blue because cooling, inspiring modesty, humility, goodness, love of truth, in short, spirituality, arouses cooling vibrations and so causing to radiate the thoughts of goodness and moral beauty. Thus color and its psychological effects, concealed in the gamut of slow, rapid, coarse and fine, super slow and coarse and super rapid and fine, play unconsciously upon our nervous system and in a powerful but invisible way, touch and influence.

CHAPTER II.

The subtile effect of color upon the nervous system and the senses is physical as well as psychological. The physical result is direct and the psychological is indirect. Involved in the psychological is an emotional as well as moral effect or influence. Any appeal of color to the senses is either agreeable or disagreeable, that is, pleasurable or painful and it is this emotional effect which is the transcendent influence that translates and carries the message of color to the mind.

Color serves many purposes. It not only acts on the nerves, as a stimulant or depressant, but serves as an ornament as well as a protection as in the case of the plumage of birds and the skins of animals. Among the fish, in temperate waters the color of the scales and skin vary from a silvery gray to a silvery brown with delicate tints of the rainbow colors intermingling, while in tropical waters, we find the most brilliant red, blue, indigo, violet, yellow, turquois and black.

The electrical and magnetic effects of the climate, heat and cold, with their stimulating and depressing influences are indicated by these colors. When nature enploys color in her creations, she has ends in view other than caprice. There is every reason for believing that color is not accidental, but a means of affording individualized forms of life their nice relations to heat and cold, light and darkness, on which all other things being equal, they largely depend, and by which their maximum of pleasure is obtained.

The great painters, Michael Angelo, DaVinci, Raphael, Murillo, used the primary colors in their pigments most effectively, and as they followed a religious canon in the use of coloration the divine blues, superb reds, royal yellows, warm browns and glorious purples and violets, conveyed spiritual ideas which the colors symbolized. Blue, as we know symbolizes truth; red, love; yellow, wisdom; brown, earthliness; purple and violet, dignity and spiritual elevation. Perhaps the medieval artists more than later painters understood the psychology of color and schemed their technique and spread their colors on canvas with this idea ever in mind. Virgin white, not only signifies cleanliness, but purity, and naturally the mind is consciously as well as unconsciously affected by it. "White as wool," "pure as ice," "chaste as snow," are sayings which convey the electrical concept of purity which is universally accepted the world over as the triune interpretation of white, while "black as sin," conveys the opposite concept. If, therefore, a color symbolist or a psychologist wishes to impress us, with purity and virtue or vice and sin, he need but hold before us the white or black, the positive or negative form of the light. He may even use scarlet, for sin has frequently been likened to scarlet, for reasons which are psychological as well as ethical; for scarlet is a stain on a white garment; and so, "Though your sins be as scarlet" (red) in case of murder or passion, "they shall be as white as wool," as in the case of the spotless purity of the lamb, or the seamless white garment of Jesus, symbolically pre-figuring the radiant glory of the Christ consciousness or the soul clothed with the ineffable light of the sun.

Vibrations were known and understood by the Ancients. Note their use in precious stones and dress.

The physical science of the light assures us that each color has a distinct frequency or vibration due to wave lengths. The red has a larger wave length than the blue, which is proportionately much shorter. That is why the grave or slow and quick notes or tones of the drum appeal to the savage or uncultivated mind. They express in sound what the red expresses in color, while the neutral notes or tones of the flute, oboe or French horn and violins, appeal to the more refined. They express in sound what the blue expresses in color.

The synchronism and synthesis of effect should be about the same in equal or similar sound and light waves by the law of proportion.

When this is understood, no one will doubt that music or color have power to soothe the savage breast.

In order to direct the student of chromopathy in a psychological analysis of color, an attempt will be made to outline in a definite way the effects of certain colors on the emotional nature. So that effects may be checked accordingly to the color influence and the student may go as far as he chooses in his experiments in a much wider experimental field which is here but vaguely indicated.

It will be perceived that what is regarded as a "temptation" and even a "sin" in certain systems of Christian theology, is due as much to

the subtile influence of color on the ?
as to human passion. Thus viole?
human nature follows an emotional co..
as certain, as grave or slow, gay or quick soun..
produce their opposite emotional effects. Of
course, to allow these physical and sense excita-
tions in the forms of vibration to influence one
against ones better nature makes the temptation
possible, but the urge to do so is often not so
much a power from within as from without.

If the psychologist wishes to pursue an exten-
sive and exhaustive investigation of the experimental phase of the subject, endless cases can
be found to prove the discovery. We have care-
lessly grown up in the midst of the riot and
chaos of color influences as to ignore their physical, subtile, moral and spiritual values. They
can be and are helps or hindrances to the spiritual life. For instance, black is the ecclesiastical or canonical color in the Christian
world for mourning. Could any color be more
depressing and illogical for a Christian Church
to accept, that teaches the hope and knowledge
of a resurrection and a life beyond death?
Black negatives all joy, hope, or expectation of
personal survival and is it not a hopeless and
hideous, though conventional spectacle of human
ignorance to wear black for mourning when, to

say the least, one should rejoice to wear white
or gray, or electric colors as blue, since the message of Jesus Christ was and is the message of
survival of the human personality after death
and in short, "the resurrection and the life"? Is
not black a rebellious contradiction and defiant
denial of what the Christian Church believes and
teaches? Then why use black? Why not em-
ploy hopeful, cheerful, stimulating colors, in-
stead of black, which is the pall and symbol of
gross ignorance, woe, evil death, non-entity?
Many Oriental nations wear violet, purple, white
and they certainly do so with more wisdom than
the Christian nations of the West.

This is but one conspicuous instance where the
color depresses one. The faith in externals
should be demonstrated by color as much as by
creed and ritual.

In the future, the psychology of color will play
a more conspicuous and conscious part in our
moral education with the distinct advantage that
when any color is displayed in dress, or interior
and exterior house decorations, each one will
know the idea or group of ideas which the colors
and color schemes convey, very much as in the
selection and arrangement of flowers for indoor
or table decoration, the Japanese ladies express

their etiquette and the subtle relationship to their guests. If anyone wishes to give warmth to an afternoon or evening house party, colors which stimulate should be chosen. Especially will this be so if the hostess is in feeble health, or has just recovered from sickness. Should one wish to appear simply modest, colors which are not dynamic but spiritual in their suggestiveness will be used in dress.

Suggestions of delicate refinement might be made by certain shades of orange, blues and violets. Amicability can be translated into pink and light blue colors, or delicate tints of violet, purple and lavenders. Elemental or primary colors often irritate a highly sensitive nature, whereas were these same natures ill, the thermal red and electrical blue, would act as gentle or powerful stimulants. While red will stimulate, blue will depress the same natures and vice versa, complimentary and neutral colors are less dynamic, but at the same time act as a buffer to the reds, blues and yellows.

CHAPTER III.

THE DICTIONARY OF COLOR MEANINGS AS PSYCHOLOGICALLY DETERMINED

Each color has a distinct vibration and nervo-
psychic reaction and registers a particular sensation. Therefore, emotionally, the sensations
produced by color can be interpreted as helpful
or harmful, pleasant or painful. Patient and
long observation has developed what may here
be designated a color dictionary. In this dictionary, human temperaments and psycho physiolog-
ical conditions are considered. While the dictionary is experimental, it is nevertheless work-
able. All colors are classified and explained under
three special heads.

1 Mental   *2 Motive*   *3 Vital*

The first are symbolized by the blues, the sec-
ond by the reds, and the third by the yellows, in
primary and complimentary forms. To attempt
to standardize any dictionary of color meanings
at this experimental stage of psychology, would
be futile and dangerous, for the reason that the

science of the psychology of color is in its infancy. It may follow, however, that the dictionary here offered which is the first of the kind attempted, may serve as a basis for the serious experimenter in this new field of psychology.

Color	*Interpretation*
Red	Love, feeling.
Yellow	Will, intuition, wisdom.
Blue	Truth, thought, intellect, spirit.
Orange	Aspiration.
Green	Immortality, growth, youth, hope.
Straw	Intuitive perception.
Turquoise	Culture, morality, spirituality, infinity, immensity.
Ecrue	Human passion, desire, earthliness.
Cafe-au-lait	Semi-consciousness, a worldly life.
Antwerp Bleu	Beauty, power, nobility, integrity.
Coffee	Indecision, materiality, attachment, sensuous consciousness and pleasure.
Purple	Royalty, Glory, Exaltation, Honor, Magnetic Attraction, Success, Truthfulness.

Drab	Potential Clairvoyance, Instinct, Genius, Precocity.
Sapphire	Spiritual perception, Realization, Loveliness.
Seal Brown	Coldness, Indifference, Repulsion, Physical Comfort.
Violet	Love of Truth and Good, Consecration, Humility, Lowliness, Divine Zeal and Earnest of Spirit.
Mauve	Spiritual Affection.
Cherry	Connubial Love and Devotion. Innocence, Harmlessness, Steadfastness, Patience, Prescience.
Salmon Pink	Ardency, Buoyancy, Exuberancy, Love of the World.
Lilac	Sweetness, Intensity, Aggressiveness, Impulsiveness.

Scarlet—Temper, Lust, Horror, Murder, Hate.

Pearl Grey—Unobtrusiveness, Shyness, Taste, Refinement, Spiritual Recognition.

Melon—Fullness of Life, Vivacity, Magnetism, Impressibility, Susceptibility.

Olive Green—Earthly, Deceitful, Treacherous, Unfaithfulness, Fear, Jealousy.

Robins Egg Blue—Faithfulness, Love of Truth, Decision, Constancy, Trust.

Pink—Gentleness, Amiability, Fondness for Friends, Pure Human Love.

Heliotrope—Seriousness, Sadness, Individuality, Loneliness.

Apple Green—Deep hope.

Nile Green—Differentiation, Change, Restlessness, Disappointment, Femininity.

Red Rose—Love of Sex, Human Love in all Natural Forms.

Lavender—Gentleness, Soberness, Subtlety, Penetration.

Magenta—Intense Humanity, Philanthropy, Devotion to Unpopular Cause or Truth, Decided Character.

Corn—Light-heartedness, Freedom of Mind, Pleasure.

Cyan Blue—Occultism, Deepness, Melancholy, Visionary.

Lemon—Love of Light, Peace, Serenity, Cheerfulness.

Claret—Moody, Distrust, Suspicion, Weakness, Passion.

Ocher—Earthly, Vehemence, Coarse Affection, and Sensual Attractions.

Peacock Blue—Repose, Self-love, Egotism, Concentration.

Canary—Sunshiny, Brightness, Love of Spiritual Things.

Gray—Clairvoyance.

Brown—Earthly.

White Rose—Silence, Power, Realization, God.

Fawn—Love of Life, Children, Nature, Helplessness.

Cardinal—P o w e r, Imperialism, Grandeur, Strength, Tyranny, Cruelty, War.

Gobelin Blue—Same as Peacock Blue, but not so Defined.

Terra Cotta—Earthly.

Buff—Perception, Sense, Reason, Judgment.

Maroon—Earthly but also Gentleness, Obdience.

Additional

Dull Pink—Same as Pink, but Wavering, Undecided, Showing Weakness.

Dark Crimson—Wickedness.

Light Blue—Sweet Reasonableness and Goodness.

Pale Greenish Blue—Spasmodic, Subtle, Impetuous.

Dark Red—Very Passionate and Earthly.

Purple—Royal in Every Sense.

Light Yellowish Brown—Hard to Please, Irritable.

Bright Red—Very Pronounced and Forward.

Orange Brown—Subtle and Worldly-wise.

Dark Brown—Diabolical, Iconoclastic, Destructive.

Pale Yellow—Little love of Life, a Mystic, Poet, Dreamer, Seer.

Dark Blue—The same as Indigo, Very Occult.

Sage Green—Lifelessness, Insanity, also Vulgarity, Coarseness, Vileness.

Light Red Purple—Love of favor, Power, Position.

Dull Orange Brown—Frailty, Faulty, Selfish.

Pale Greenish Blue—Uniform Feeling, but Easily Disturbed, Circumstantial.

Golden Brown—Maturity, Old Age, Decay.

Dull Bluish Pink—Fickleness, Inconstancy, a Flirt or Coquette.

Brown—Earthly.

Dark Red Brown—Very Disagreeable.

Bluish Pink—Delightfully Entertaining, Evenly Balanced, A Favorite.

Dark Green—Hate, Envy, Jealousy, Spite.

Dull Orange—Adolescent Understanding, Youthful, Love of Life.

Leather—Roughness, Coarseness, Obstinacy.

Deep Rose Pink—Devotion to the Personal and Constancy of Love.

Gray Blue—Depressed Spirits.

Emerald Green—Same as Pure Green.

Lead Color—Psychic Power and Expression.

Dark Red—Malevolent.

Purplish Black—Black Magic, Necromancy.

Purplish White—White Magic, Leucomancy.

Neutral Grey—A Mediator, Meditation, Reconciliation, Justification.

This tabulation is incomplete because it is merely suggestive and not final. Meditation and observation will lead to precise and unfailing definitions and psycho therapeutic generalizations. Both color and music arouse as well as stimulate the memory, imagination and ideality There is no magic about the co-ordination between color and nervo psychic susceptibility. In a very subtile as well subtle way the soul responds to color, but the appeal is first to the eye, then to the perception and afterward to the soul. The subjective possibility of color is limitless. One can mentally visualize and telepath color to a recipient and produce the same results as objective color. As this phase of the subject is understood, far reaching benefits will be obtained; even color blindness will be no barrier to the mental process. The effort is certain, because a subjective influence on the imagination. Man's resourcefulness grows as he enters the larger and illimitable field of his psychic and divine potentalities.

CHAPTER IV.

Color in the Nursery as a Moral and Corrective Agency

The nursery is the chrysalis, into which the child fashions its moral and spiritual tendencies and habits, and from which it should emerge as a butterfly, ready for the new life in the outside world. The nursery should never become even in thought or fact, a penitentiary for the children. Nothing harms a child more than repression. To punish it, by confining it in a nursery is to subvert the ideal and actual function of the nursery and condemn it in the child's mind as a place of unhappy dreams and unpleasant recollections. The nursery as a room, should be the most welcome and inviting chamber in the house and next to mother's arms and father's knees, should be the sweetest and holiest of places. To hurry or drag a child after committing an error or indiscretion into the nursery, and there after locking the door, forcing it to remain under threat of a more severe punishment, is to condemn it (to the child's imagination) and rob it of its charm and atmosphere.

Children are more often abused than understood by parents and even nurses and governesses. And the nursery is chosen as a short cut to obedience, because of a lack of the knowledge of child psychology. A Doctor of Divinity, after observing the behavior of certain children asked the mother how she ever brought her children up (there were six of them) to be so obedient and so well behaved and she answered, "by not sparing the rod." It is doubtful, if the rod was necessary, and today, in the best and most cultivated families, the rod would be regarded as a weapon of barbarism, if not of cruelty to animals. And mothers and fathers who today punish their children to force them into obedience, who box their ears and slap their faces or jerk their arms, for a misdemeanor, surely needed to learn before marriage, the higher law of love, before they ever dared to bring children into the world. A child is a potential angel.

If abnormal or subnormal, the child needs the wisest and most tender care in a private or public institution, for while the angel is there, either the brain or nervo psychic organism is deranged and unbalanced, and it would be brutality and cruelty to punish them. To keep them from harming themselves and others is necessary, but no thought of punishment should enter into their treatment. If the child is a potential angel, resembling in perfect spirit the sweet little cherubs which Raphael, Angelo and da Vinci depicted in many of their masterpieces, it brings with it into its earthly atmosphere and habitation, "trailing clouds of glory" as Wordsworth beautifully expressed it, which should be respected even if not sensed by hard headed and materially minded parents.

Perhaps the colors which suggest this atmosphere, and rare state of psychic expression in an etherial world, are most appealing to children, as has been discovered by patient and long observations by psychological and lay experts, because they intuitively feel their influence and perceive their message. Reds, blues, yellows, greens, browns, purples, violets, strike the child's eyes because most obtrusive and dynamic, but the softer and delicate tints and shades of pink, light blue, turquoise, amber, gray and green, are more subtile and the psychological reactions more interior and spiritual. Primary colors produce effects or results almost instantaneously, while complementary colors work more slowly. A practical suggestion, although a novel one, is to have curtains made of certain seven or ten colors which could be rolled down from their poles at the top of the ceilings of the nursery, changing the color scheme of the wall paper, whatever it is (and originally it should always be either a pink or light blue figured or flowered paper), entirely covering the entire four walls attaching the same at the base. As nurseries are small rooms, the expense for such curtains would be commensurate with the purse. These curtains could be made of a tough paper, or window shade cloth, which would resist wear. These curtains could be made according to a psychological scheme which will be given, under that branch of Psychological Pathology known as chromopathic psychology, and should be made to entertain the child's mind with affirmative and never with negative colors as black or grays, although of course they have their beneficient uses as the darkness, when the child is put to sleep, which suggests absence and forgetfulness of light and of physical objects.

Chromopathic Psychology

1   Red.—Excites, Stimulates Love and Pleasure and Overcomes Hate. For children who are peevish, weak and nervous. A vitalizer.

2   Blue—Stimulates or Excites Truth and Overcomes Falsification, an Exaggerated Ego, Selfishness, Overeating, all Indulgences and Passions, as Anger. For Sleepless Children.

3   Yellow. Excites or Stimulates the Will, Obedience, and is for Disobedient, Incorrigible Children. A Color Gloriously Adapted to Sensitive, Intuitive Children, Who Love to be alone. Helps to Overcome Timidity and bashfulness, Shyness.

4   Pink.—Excites or Stimulates Hope, Joy, Amiability, Frendliness and overcomes Ugliness and Distemper, Lack of Sociability. Antidote for Blues.

5   Light Blue.—Excites and Stimulates Spirituality, Fondness for Books, Friends, Love of Truth, Neatness, Honesty, Faith, Order, Harmony, Music.

6. Violet.—Stimulates the Will and the Moral Nature, to Soothe and Comfort, to Arouse Conscience, to Act as a Spiritual Tonic.

7 Purple.—Arouses a Sense of Dignity, Self Respect, to Impress Reverence and Veneration. Can be substituted for blue among older children.

8 Green.—In lighter shades, Stimulates the Emotion of Life, Energy, Vitality, Youth, Immortality. Offers a Relief to tired eyes and nerves and therefore is a tonic for any nervous or mental disorder.

9 White—Not a Color, of course, but can be used to suggest Purity, Wholeness, Sincerity, Divinity, Perfection.

10 Brown.—Suggests Earthliness, Matter, Nature, Life in the Fields and Wood and is valuable for Children who are Restless to go out of doors and who on rainy days need a color adaptable to the weather.

The scheme as here suggested is but a bare outline of what may, in practice, prove enormously helpful in results. For the efficacy of chromopathic psychology is in its silent rather than visible appeal. No audible counsel or advice need be offered to the recipient. The color offers its own motto, counsel, sermon, magic. It is felt and psychically absorbed. The eyes, the windows of the soul, reflect the colors of the soul, and as plants absorb sunshine, indeed the whole gamut of color contained in the light, so the soul, on the physical plane, a human plant growing in the garden of the world, absorbs its vitalizing, therapeutic and nervo psychic stimulus from the colors.

Children need such beneficent and corrective influence far more than advice, reprimands or punishment, and as they receive such subtle influences, duty and obedience now the two most hated words in the vocabulary of childhood, will take on new and inspiring meanings under color alchemy. Alchemy indeed it is and magic too, as these two words embody spiritual power, usually not associated with chemistry, or physics, but a magic and alchemy, not involving any sense of the supernatural or the infringement of Law, but results of a higher and finer order.

Parents will do well to observe a patience under the experimental use of color, and not betray a doubt of the result, nor show any violent emotion as anger or use any physical force, when conducting a child into the nursery when the need for its chromopathic power is felt. Parents need to share with their children the chromopathic uses to which the nursery is put, and indeed, its profit cannot be exaggerated. For it is often found that parents, rather than children are often to blame for the temporary disposition and ugly behavior of their offspring. The posture of the child while in the nursery need never be that of attention or first position. The child should be placed in the nursery to be free and at ease, to play and enjoy itself, and should never enter this sanctuary without its consent. Nor should it be coaxed or teased into going into it. The true way is to lead the way by lovingly obtaining the child's consent, and this can usually be done by any true and wise parent.

CHAPTER V.

"TEMPERAMENTAL" COLORS AND THEIR PSYCHIC REAGENCIES AND REACTIONS. PSYCHOPATHIC INFLUENCE OF COLOR

What is meant by "temperamental" colors are the colors which are likely to appeal to ones nature. Each one has a certain makeup or constitution. It has been found that "temperaments" may be grouped under certain heads and necessarily fall into certain categories. There are the religious, literary, musical or artistic and scientific temperaments, and each one may be defined by the colors, blue, light blue, pink and orange or yellow. Speaking of nationalism, the national spirit and the national color, blue symbolizes the Jew, Parsee, Mohammedan, Hindu and pre-eminently the "religious" temperament, because it stands for Truth, Spirit, God and the spiritual life.

Pink or red symbolizes Greek and Latin nations, as the Italian and French, pre-eminently typify the "artistic" temperament, because it symbolizes love, the affections, humanity, deeds of heroic valor. Light blue symbolizes the British and American nations and pre-eminently the "literary" temperament, because it stands for knowledge and life, freedom, fraternity, happiness.

Yellow or orange symbolizes the will, the highest function and power of our nature, and pre-eminently typifies the "scientific" temperament.

There are exceptions to all classifications, for groups of individuals or of nations can symbolize both the composite, religious and literary, the literary and musical, the musical and religious or the scientific and literary temperaments. All classification should be elastic and general, rather than fixed and arbitrary.

No attempt is made to put nations into such categories as are indicated by the colors of their flags. These flags standardize certain political ideals, rather than national traits, or temperamental likes or dislikes.

The law of attraction is broadly shown in these temperamental attractions to certain colors or groups of colors. For instance, the blues would favor gradation of blue where white is predominant as violets, gray blue, Italian blue and turquoise, but would disfavor its compliments as red or yellow and its contrasts as orange.

The reds would favor gradations of red as pink, grey pink, purple, but would disfavor its complements as blue or yellow and its contrasts as green. The yellows would favor gradations of yellow as canary, orange, chrome, but would disfavor its complements as red and blue, and its contrasts as purple. This law is chemical as well as psychological and our natural constitution thus plays in a field of light, selecting such colors as please it. It would be a strange and unnatural world, if this were not so.

*Contrasting and complementary colors often act as chemical and psychopathic re-agents. Not only do they reveal the nature of the action of other colors, but they supply under excess or lack, what the sick need. Such colors however disagreeable under normal conditions, act as stimulants or depressants when the nervo psychic constitution is disordered.

---

* Dr. Babbitt discovered that one can know the harmonic contrast of color by its complement, red forming a contrast with yellow and blue, which is green, and yellow forming a contrast with red and blue, which is orange.

Were this a technical work on chromopathy, much more could be written along these lines. Suffice it to say that Dr. E. D. Babbitt has comprehended the field most thoroughly in his splendid book entitled "The Principles of Light and Color." This much may be added, however, that magnetic colors as the reds are thermal, and stimulating, the electrical colors, as the blues, are chemical and cooling, and in cases of headache, insanity, fever, the blues and violets should be used, while in cases of tuberculosis, paralysis, melancholia, loneliness, debility, the reds and purples should be employed.

From a purely psychological standpoint, along lines of psycho-therapy, red and pinks excite hope, inspire optimism and so neutralize the results or reactions of fear, distrust, despair, while the blues and violets increase a fondness for books, stimulate a love of intellectual, scientific and spiritual pursuits, and so neutralize the results of materialism in all of its forms.

In conclusion it can be said that the artistic temperament is balanced and neutralized best by the colors, which appeal to the religious temperament and vice versa, as the scientific and musical temperaments find their balance and neutrality in the artistic and religious, with whom they are in more or less of conjunction as well as opposition.

CHAPTER VI.

COLOR IN DRESS. WHY BRIDES WEAR WHITE AND MOURNERS BLACK. INTERNATIONAL CUSTOMS ANALYZED

The primary colors of red, yellow and blue, appealed to the elemental and simple minds of the savage, because their vibrations were the most physical in their effects on their senses. Reds are warm, blues are cooling, while yellow is more or less neutral. The ruddy reds of the earth, the rosy sunrises and sunsets and the fierce flames of fire, and the blue of water and sky, strangely impressed the early peoples. So, from sun and fire, they learned that the red symbolizes heat and they used yellow and red pygmies, yellow and red feathers and yellow and red garments, not only because they liked them as ornaments, but because they imitated nature in her elementary moods. The blues were not so commonly used because less dynamic and violent, but were featured by the Jews, Egyptians, Arabs and the Orientals, in their tapes-

tries, robes, portieres, frescoes and ecclesiastical
vestments. The subtle reason for this is its
spiritual and mental rather than emotional appeal to the senses. This was not due to a lack
of dyes, as it is a well known fact, fully corrob-
orated by Wendell Phillips in his celebrated
oration on "The Lost Arts," that dyes were
known, as for instance the royal or Tyrian purple, thousands of years before Christ, which art
has since been lost. This was not only true of
Phoenecia, Egypt, Assyria, but of· Persia and
India. The less bizarre and spectacular colors, as
the gray blues, gray pinks, grays, gray purples
and violets, fawn browns, yellows and greens
were used in the Mural decorations of temples
and the costumes of the women of royalty.* They
had developed a high, fascinating and unexcelled
artistry in color combinations which the modern
world has not surpassed. And the most remarkable part of their use of color was their psychological knowledge of its spiritual values and the
subtile effect of color on the individual. In fact,
color, among the Eastern nations, was a function
of religion, and the priests established, sanction-
ed and supported the function as long as they
were in power.

---

*Artistic evidences of Egyptian fondness for subdued tones can be
seen in the Museum at Cairo, also in the ruins of their temples on
the Nile.

The reason why brides wear white, is the same which caused the Vestal Virgins among Greeks and Romans to wear a white flowing gown, centuries before Christianity dawned upon the world. White typifies innocence, virginity, chastity, without a stain, blemish or spot. It is, therefore, the fitting color (or absence of color) emblematic of maidenhood or virginity. This is too evident to need further comment.

Black, on the other hand, typifies the universal negative, in which color is absorbed, hid and not manifest, and is emblematic of death, matter, oblivion, annihilation, nothing—loss of life and love. It therefore conveys no idea or thought of immortality or survival of the personality of death, and its effect upon human nature is depressing, joyless, sad, reproachful, hostile, evil.

In analyzing international habits and customs of mourning, a criticism is made against the time honored Christian fashion and precedent, which have been blindly followed by society, out of a loyal and sincere wish to pay the last sad respects to the dead; for the simple reason that such solemn respect should not spiritually and rationally be associated with black.

As a Christian nation, believing in, if not able to know and prove the survival of the soul at death, black symbolizes a *denial of the resurrection* and an infamous repudiation of the affirmation of Jesus, "I am the Resurrection and the Life," and "I came that ye might have life and have it more abundantly." It typifies faithlessness, blindness, death, annihilation, agnosticism, atheism, materialism. It takes the divinity out of the shield of the Christian Religion and throws a pall over the crown of life. It deliberately, as though designed by the arch enemy of truth, crushes the soul, by screening and camouflaging its vision with the darkest, blackest clouds of nescience and ignorance. A fashion, which should be more honored in the breach than in the observance, simply because a false theology has made the Christian world falsely believe that the body and soul sleep together in the grave until doomsday, whereas the soul is liberated instantly at death, no better, no worse in character because of death, but free of the body, yet held by the life it lived on earth, to its attractions and attachments, its karma, the planes and spheres of thought and action in the Spirit World. Therefore, any revolutionary tendencies to change the fashionable color of mourning, should be hailed as a contribution to an enlightened public conscience and intelligence.

Purple, violet, gray, white could be used with

no suggestion of error or evil, but with beneficent effect. White especially, as hinting at the
light, and suggesting however remotely, the
spirit's triumph over darkness and evil, would
be preferable to other colors, however nationaliz-
ed by both tradition and custom. White is the
opposite of black, and as black typifies negation
of life, white symbolizes positiveness of life.

This idea is a religious and scientific one of
survival, is important to teach and impress sol-
emnly upon a none too spiritually minded gener-
ation, because it follows that if black, symboliz-
ing death, evil and non existence is allowed to
continue to be the formal and popular color of
mourning, the fact of the soul's survival, will
expose our self elected ignorance and rebuke our
time honored stupidity. As a matter of fact, the
correct idea of death has made inroads upon
foolish western customs of mourning. In some
quarters, black has been discarded altogether,
as has black crepe on doors and evergreen and
flowers substituted in its place. It would go a
great way toward educating the masses in the
spiritual significance of death, if the corpse was
robed in white and placed in white coffins in-
stead of black, irrespective of age, and clergy-
men taught from pulpits and in homes and when
ever opportunity suggested the need, that white

preaches the best sort of a mute but comforting sermon on the resurrection. As the dawn announces the rising of the sun and the advent of day, so white announces the fact that death has lost its sting and the grave its victory. This is the truest orthodox Christian teaching, however heterodox it may seem from an ecclesiastical and theological standpoint.

In Europe and England, the habit of mourning among men and women is still black, the custom being in part Roman, but under the Roman Empire, white was worn by the women and black by the men. The color of mourning in Turkey is violet, in Egypt yellow, and in China, white. Ecclesiastical, and sometimes civil authority fixes the color. Now in this age of science and democracy, the custom of wearing black will be more honored in the breach than in the observance, and sane, rational and spiritual ideals, founded on the facts of a demonstrable immortality will popularize white, perhaps adding color as one may be led, but discarding forever the black.

Purple, violet, yellow, white, even blue have spiritual significance and are vitalizing, stimulating and never depressing.

Brides are married in white and carry white blossoms because white is the perfect symbol of virginity, innocence and chastity. It lifts maidenhood and womankind by the sheer appeal to the senses above the slightest cloud of material suggestion of worldliness or earthliness, and translates her into the garden of paradise.

As the Epiphany marks the earth's investment of light and occurs twelve days after Christmas, which heralds the actual rebirth of the New Year, the ascent of the sun to the vernal equinox, so the bride who goes forth to be married to the bridegroom, takes on the light of this new life.

The psychological effect of white on the bridegroom should be reflective of his spiritual station and dignity and will be in fact, when man gives to woman what woman gives to man and when social laws and customs demand and grant equal rights and privileges before the law. When the integrity and unity of life is at last recognized from matter to spirit and from the crystal to God and all vibrations are registered and realized, color will be found to have its value in the psychology of life, and it will not appear as a mere accident or coincidence of natural phenomena, but a service in the divine scheme of things.

Dr. J. C. F. Grumbine's Books

"Child Psychology"—That Wonderfully helpful book—a boon to mothers and fathers—now ready_____Paper   .75

"The Psychology of Color"—a unique and fascinating book. _____ Paper   .75

"Concentration"—Key to Success, Power and Mastery _____ Paper   .75

"Telepathy"—How to send radiograms. Teaches science of thought transference_____Cloth $1.60 Paper $ .75

"Auras and Colors"—With dictionary of color meanings Wonderful book. Tenth edition_____Paper   .75

"Beckoning Hands from the Near Beyond"—Most comforting book _____Cloth 1.60

"The Spirit World"—Where and what it is. A revelation _____ Paper   .50

"Boston Lectures on the New Psychology"—Excellent text book _____Cloth 1.60

"Clairvoyance"—First practical text book ever written on the subject. Teaches how to penetrate the veil of sense, commune consciously with departed loved ones, how to realize the cosmic or divine consciousness. Cloth 1.60

"Clairaudience"—Teaches how to hear the whisperings of the spirit people. Sane and practical in technique _____ Paper   .75

"Psychometry"—The sixth sense. The divine sense of common things. Best book on subject. Teaches the science _____ Paper   .50

"Easy Lessons in Occult Science"_____Paper   .50

"Melchizedek"—A revelation and key to Bible mysteries Unorthodox but canonical_____Cloth $1.00 Paper   .75

"The New Thought Religion"—The first constructive broad book written on the subject_____Paper   .50

PRESS NOTICES

"It is questionable if Dr. Grumbine's superior, for the past thirty years at least, has been on the platform."—Harbinger of Light, Melbourne, Australia.

"He possesses a complete mastery over his subject."—Western Australian, Perth.

Send Moneys to DR. J. C. F. GRUMBINE, Station E, Cleveland, Ohio

CPSIA information can be obtained at www.ICGtesting.com
Printed in the USA
LVOW02s1148180713

343500LV00005B/430/P